SCHIRMER'S LIBRARY
OF MUSICAL CLASSICS

Vol. 2008

EDVARD GRIEG

"Peer Gynt" Suite
Complete

For Piano

ISBN 978-0-7935-4517-9

G. SCHIRMER, Inc.

DISTRIBUTED BY

HAL•LEONARD®
CORPORATION
7777 W. BLUEMOUND RD. P.O. BOX 13819 MILWAUKEE, WI 53213

CONTENTS

Morgenstimmung.
(Morning-mood.)

Edited and fingered by
Louis Oesterle

EDVARD GRIEG. Op. 46, № 1.

Allegretto pastorale (♩ = 60)

Åse's Death

Edited and fingered by
Louis Oesterle

Edvard Grieg. Op. 46, № 2

Andante doloroso (♩=50)

Anitra's Tanz.
(Dance of Anitra.)

Edited and fingered by
Louis Oesterle.

Tempo di Mazurka (♩=160)

EDVARD GRIEG. Op. 46, № 3.

*) Trills without afterbeat.

8

In der Halle des Bergkönigs.
(In the Hall of the Mountain-king.)

Edited and fingered by
Louis Oesterle.

Alla marcia e molto marcato (♩ = 138)

EDVARD GRIEG. Op. 46, No 4.

Suite

I

Rape of the Bride   Ingrid's Plaint

Edvard Grieg. Op. 55

II

Arab Dance

Allegretto vivace

III
Peer Gynt's Homecoming
(Stormy evening on the coast)

* 𝄚𝄚𝄚𝄚𝄚 𝄚𝄚𝄚𝄚 etc.

attacca

IV
Solvejg's Song

Allegretto, tranquillamente

poco rit.

Andante